SYSTEMS SCALE

EIGHT SIMPLE SYSTEMS THAT IGNITE GROWTH

BRETT A. BLAKE

Author of
RENEWAL: Leading Direct Selling Turnarounds
and
Private Equity Investing in Direct Selling:
Identifying Risks & Rewards

Systems Scale: Eight Simple Systems That Ignite Growth
© 2020 Brett A. Blake. All rights reserved.

ISBN-13: 978-1-7333568-5-5

No part of this publication may be reproduced or transmitted in any form or by any means, mechanical or electronic, including photocopying and recording, or by any information storage and retrieval system, without permission in writing from author or publisher (except by a reviewer, who may quote brief passages and/or show brief video clips in a review).

CONTENTS

Preface	v
Introduction	ix
Chapter 1: Systems are the Secret	13
Chapter 2: The Eight Systems That Ignite Growth	21
Chapter 3: Customer Acquisition System	31
Chapter 4: Recruiting Customers to Be New Distributors	41
Chapter 5: New Distributor Success System	47
Chapter 6: Distributor Advancement or ROI Rank System	53
Chapter 7: Convention Attendance System	59
Chapter 8: Communications System	63
Chapter 9: Leadership Development & Training Systems	67
Chapter 10: Recognition System	73
Chapter 11: Launching New Systems	77
Chapter 12: Managing with Systems	85
Acknowledgments	93
About the Author	95

PREFACE

On October 14, 2019, my daughter and I were enjoying the last day of her fall break with a friendly bowling match. As she picked up the bowling ball to take her first turn, I noticed an incoming phone call with a number I recognized. It was the phone number of the Church of Jesus Christ of Latter-day Saints headquarters in Salt Lake City, Utah, a number I remembered from having interned in the Church's Public Affairs department thirty years ago.

Instinctively, I picked up my phone and answered the phone call. The voice on the other end of the phone said, "Brother Blake, I am the assistant to Elder Quentin L Cook, are you sitting down?"

"No," I said.

"You might want to," she said. "This is good news, at least I think it is, but you probably want to sit down."

I apologized for the loud noise in the background and told her I was bowling with my daughter, and then she said, "Could you and your wife meet with Elder Cook by video conference on Wednesday?"

I know Elder Quentin L Cook to be an Apostle of Jesus Christ, a modern-day witness of the Savior and a leader of the Church of Jesus

Christ of Latter-day Saints. Therefore, you will understand me when I say that her question left me with no strength in my legs and with a pale face. I was glad to be sitting.

I was about to say yes when I realized I had a flight booked Wednesday afternoon to travel to a SUCCESS Partners' CEO Summit in Santa Monica, California, so I said, "I have a flight that day, let me just check and see what time that flight is." I looked at my phone and went to pull up my flight information and thought, 'wait a minute, this is an Apostle who wants to meet with us, I can change any flight and accommodate his schedule.'

I put the phone back to my face and said, "Yes, that will work."

She gave me some details and confirmed that Erin would be with me and then said goodbye.

Kate had been bowling her turn during the short call and now was standing in front of me, and I was crying. She said, "Dad, what is happening?" I couldn't think of anything to say to Kate other than the truth, so I told her, "Kate that was the assistant to an Apostle. She asked if mom and I would meet with Elder Cook on Wednesday." Somehow, ten-year-old Kate knew what that meant, and the rest of the night, we played lots of games, played on a ropes course, a game of billiards, but our conversation kept returning to the call. At one point, Kate hugged me and said, "Dad, I don't want to serve a mission right now."

After telling Kate, I called Erin and told her. She believed me immediately and began to cry. We both knew that this call would change our life and that it was the beginning of what would be an invitation to leave our profession, one I have loved and worked in for nearly a quarter-century. After the meeting with Elder Cook and a second videoconference with President Dallin H Oaks, we received a call to serve as mission leaders in the Colorado Denver North Mission for three years starting in July of 2020. We will have the opportunity to care for more than 180 young missionaries serving in the Denver and Boulder areas. We will be volunteers, devoting 100% of our time to the work, and will rent our home and sell most of our other belongings (cars, boat, etc.) before we go.

As I have thought about leaving my career for at least three years, I have felt an urgency to share what I have learned, particularly the content of this book. While I recognized the industry has a short-term need for the content of the companion volumes I wrote on *RENEWAL*, I believe the most valuable content I could share will be found in this short book on systems. I'm grateful for the help of the team at SUCCESS Partners, who encouraged me and have helped me publish this final book before I leave.

I've also felt a desire to share my perspective on the direct selling industry, which continues to receive criticism from news media and social media sources. I acknowledge that the industry has had bad actors and that the inexperience of most of our new distributors lends itself to awkward social moments. However, I have seen so many positive life experiences, so much personal development, and the positive results of the economic opportunities afforded to direct sellers.

I confess to being more than a little irritated by young people who take to social media as critics of the industry. I'm especially annoyed by those who have grown up in wealth (even middle-class wealth) and have never wanted for the basics of life. These silver spoon critics use social media to ridicule those who are willing to do hard things in return for a chance to experience things that their upbringing never afforded them.

Rather than being annoyed when a friend chooses to try and make ends meet as a salesperson for a product they like, wouldn't a good friend embrace the opportunity to help that friend? Most of us would gladly offer a 'gift' to a friend in need. So why would we allow ourselves to feel uneasy when our friend instead tries to earn money by selling something they believe has value? Is it too much to ask that a friend buy something from us, even if it isn't the least expensive, or might even be something we don't really need?

Friends help friends and should be willing to support their friends' efforts to improve their life and the future of their families.

Should we be more product-focused and customer-focused and less opportunity and recruiting focused? "Yes!"

Should we offer products with great value? "Yes!"

There is room for improvement, and as someone who has spent two decades in the boardrooms and back rooms of dozens of companies, I can honestly say that the companies in this channel are making progress. I believe this book will help.

As I prepare to step away from the channel and people I have come to love, I offer this work and with it, my simple "thank you" to all of the wonderful field leaders and corporate executives who have made my career so fulfilling.

I believe that direct selling is at an inflection point. Never has the market been so open to the idea of purchasing from solo entrepreneurs. Never has the technology been so available to even the playing field so an individual can compete with a Fortune 50 company. The demand is enormous, and the opportunity for growth is unlimited. I suspect that I will return to find direct selling companies many times their current size and perhaps to find that today's large consumer brands are participating in the channel in some way.

Now is the time for companies to learn how to employ systems to scale their direct selling business. I hope that means you and your company.

INTRODUCTION

I began my career in direct selling in 1990 as a young executive for Melaleuca, Inc. Since that start, I've had the opportunity to serve as a senior executive for six companies, to consult for several more and to study dozens of successes and failures. However, it took me nearly thirty years to discover the eight systems I will share with you in the pages that follow.

I actually learned the power of systems as we grew Beachbody's direct selling business by 10x in just three years and then to nearly a billion dollars in the next three years. Despite the success we had employing systems at Beachbody, I made the mistake of thinking that a single system was sufficient—it was certainly sufficient for those years of hypergrowth. I now realize that assumption was a limiting mistake.

Before we talk about the eight secrets, or the eight systems you will want to exploit to ignite your company's growth, let's begin with an introduction to the concept of systems and make sure you and I share the same definition.

Most of us like to hear and want to believe that people are the most important asset of a company. It seems like I was taught in my very first business class that good people are the key to success in business. We hear experts like management consultant James Kerr say, "The people in your company will ultimately determine the success or failure of your business,"[1] and we begin nodding our head in violent agreement.

This fact was drilled so deeply into my management mind that it came as a jaw-dropping, head-scratching shock to learn that McDonald's was founded based on the founders' virtual surrender to their belief that they wouldn't be able to consistently hire good people. According to Michael Gerber's account of the founding of McDonald's in his book *The E-Myth Revisited*, the McDonald's founders Richard and Maurice McDonald realized that they could not attract excellent workers to help them in their restaurant. That realization was in part the driver behind their decision to close down their first restaurant and to completely start over. This time they redesigned their operations to allow below-average employees to produce consistently high-quality products. Ray Kroc eventually discovered the brilliance of that philosophy, and the golden arches have become one of the most recognizable brands in the world.

The idea of creating systems that others could duplicate to deliver a consistently high-quality product gave birth to the Franchise industry. That industry, built on the effective use of systems, has grown to account for approximately 3% of the U.S. economy, producing an impressive estimated annual output of $787.5 billion (in 2019) in the U.S. alone. The success of franchising is even more noteworthy when it is compared to the $35.4 billion in direct selling output reported for 2019.

There are many variables that account for the significantly higher output of franchising, but one of the key variables is the industry's focus on using systems to make success in their business predictable. Franchise businesses use systems for almost everything they do. Systems are deployed to create a perfect Big Mac and to ensure

---
1 https://www.inc.com/james-kerr/your-people-are-your-most-important-asset.html

marvelous marketing and to assure accurate accounting. Franchise owners and their independent franchise entrepreneurs are equally committed to producing and perfecting systems that are good enough to make even teenagers successful. They've learned that perfect systems can make below-average people extraordinarily successful.

Franchisers know that you can plug anyone into a great system, and they will succeed. Because great people are hard to find and harder to afford, franchisers have learned that you can scale with great systems faster than you can scale with great people.

Too many direct selling companies focus on great products, excellent compensation systems, and eye-popping marketing and neglect the difficult work of making their customer acquisition system something that is simple enough to ensure the success of below-average distributors. Don't take your eye off my point by assuming I'm encouraging you to ignore great people or not even aspire to have great people. That is not the point. The point is that you need systems that great people can blow up and that below-average people can also use to run a profitable business.

If there is any industry or channel that needs great systems, it is direct selling. Why? Because they encourage new distributors to start part-time while they are focusing full-time on another job and often living a full life outside of work. I think you will agree that even amazing people have a tough time sustaining extraordinary results when they are not able to focus on just one thing. How do you overcome the requirement of having to rely on part-time people? You create simple systems that anyone can follow.

Remember that during periods of growth, a majority of the distributors that belong to a company are likely relatively new. These new distributors are at the peak of their excitement but have no skills and no experience to assure success. The key to overcoming this paradox is the use of a system and/or tools that reduce the need for significant training or skills. Great tools allow a brand-new distributor to produce as though they were an expert with years of experience.

IF YOU'VE GROWN, YOU HAVE A CUSTOMER ACQUISITION SYSTEM

I believe that every great success in direct selling can be traced to the use of a simple system. Some systems are based on a short-term truth—"we are growing like crazy": others become worn out and the field becomes fatigued by their constant use. Systems have different life cycles, and sales results tend to follow those life cycles, but the thoughtful student of direct selling history will be able to attribute systems to success.

In a phone call with the CEO of a struggling direct selling company, I asked her what the company's customer acquisition system was during the company's peak growth.

"That's the problem," she said. "We don't have a system and never have had a system!"

I knew this company had experienced significant growth, and I now know that growth doesn't happen without a system. I didn't take the time that afternoon to convince this CEO of that fact that her company had once grown with the help of a system. However, I do hope to convince you in this book that your company has or should have eight systems, and they shouldn't be a secret to you or to any member of your staff.

CHAPTER 1:
SYSTEMS ARE THE SECRET

Every successful direct selling company has a customer acquisition system, but surprisingly few executives understand what systems their field is using to grow their business. That is a bold claim, but years of experience in company after company gives me great confidence in making that statement. Thus, systems are a secret—at least to most direct selling executives.

How can a company have success and not understand the system that is generating its sales? Often the system driving sales is discovered by the independent sales field leaders. Their experience of trial and error and try again, along with their everyday connection with customers, provides them the perfect opportunity to create, refine and perfect a system of sales.

Shockingly few companies have taken the time to learn exactly what their field leaders are using to generate sales. Because so few executives focus on systems, for many (perhaps most) companies, the independent field leaders define the company's systems and teach their teams with little or no support from the company.

One company that didn't initially understand the customer acquisition system developed in the field is Herbalife. One of the company's waves of success in the United States came as a result of a program developed in Mexico. Rather than attempting to sell a monthly supply of their leading product, Formula 1®, Herbalife's distributors in Mexico offered single servings from their home or workplace and called them "Nutrition Clubs." At first, Herbalife's executives reportedly didn't understand the program and even tried to prevent it from being taught in the U.S. despite the fact that it worked in the Latino communities. Fortunately for Herbalife, they were not successful in stopping this practice and eventually were forced to accept it. I'm told by former executives that Herbalife's impressive growth in the U.S. Latino community started as a result of this distributor-led customer acquisition system that was imported from Mexico by field leaders, and then eventually embraced and supported by the corporate team in the United States.

In the spring of 2017, Nu Skin had a sudden and unexpected revival of sales in the United States. Despite the company's impressive investment in research and development and significant corporate efforts to increase sales, the new sales surge came from an almost forgotten product Nu Skin had been selling for more than ten years. Why? Led by the success of a new distributor in the United Kingdom and follow-on success by a new distributor in the U.S., Nu Skin's field leaders learned how to use social media to share before and after pictures of their decade-old AP 24® Whitening Fluoride Toothpaste to drive demand and increase sales.

Nu Skin executives were wise enough to set aside other initiatives and align behind the momentum of both the product and the social sharing method of selling. The company has followed its field to deploy tech tools designed to support the simple system. As is so often the case, Nu Skin's selling system was accidentally discovered by distributors with a combined tenure of fewer than six months with the company. To the credit of Nu Skin's management team, they were astute enough to recognize and capitalize on the system and reap its benefits.

SALES SYSTEMS CAN LEAD TO SALES DECLINE

Often senior marketing executives have no real field experience, and while they understand much about direct selling, they have never taken the time to understand the compensation system. I can make this claim because I started my career as the senior marketing executive at USANA Health Sciences and tried to get by without understanding the compensation plan for many months. I was afraid to ask for help because I thought that field leaders would be shocked to learn of my ignorance in something so important to them. So, I continued to avoid deep dive learning sessions with successful field leaders. Now I know that I was not only ignorant about how distributors were paid, but I was also flying blind without an understanding of how our products were actually being sold to customers and how new distributors were being recruited. I've since learned that I was not alone. Many executives continue to have the same experience.

Years later, as a senior executive at Beachbody, I came to understand the cost of my ignorance. When company executives don't truly understand the field's tactics and needs, they waste much of their marketing budget creating tools that never get used or even worse, new products that actually work against the selling system (more about that later). In fact, the tools often confuse new distributors who are being taught how to sell using one system and are given tools by the company that clearly would be used to support another way of selling. The result: new distributors often do nothing, and growth slows.

Misfit sales tools created by a company ignorant of its field's selling system also serve to divide corporate executives from field leaders. Why? Field leaders who want to be seen as being loyal put on a grateful face when tools are introduced, and then out of fear of being labeled as a rebel, they hide their training and system even further from the company executives, thus perpetuating the cycle of misunderstanding.

Company after company has seen their growth slow and spiral down because executives have made changes to their pricing, product offerings or messaging that inadvertently disrupted the selling system the field was using with success. Even Beachbody saw its growth slow when the company's new digital platform was first introduced without proper consideration given to its impact on the economics and recurring revenue of Team Beachbody Coaches.

Another example of a disconnect between corporate and the field selling system is the rise and fall of skincare direct seller Arbonne. Arbonne had experienced hockey stick growth as a result of its field's selling system. Field leaders taught their teams to drop off a full skincare system to prospects with this offer:

"I want you to try this amazing product line, and I'm so confident you're going to love this that I'm going to allow you to try it for a week. If you love it, which I think you will, I'm going to stop by next week to pick up a check. If you don't like it, I'll pick up the product, and you owe me nothing."

Arbonne's selling system worked and gave new customers and new distributors immediate confidence in the quality of the product. The company grew to more than $800 million in annual sales, but reportedly, their private equity investors followed counsel they received from a consultant with little field experience and a conservative CFO and decided the system was too risky. Investors demanded that the executive team stop the practice. The result was tragic. The company began a free fall that didn't end until sales had dropped to less than 50% of their peak. In 2009, Arbonne reported sales of just $270 million. Only bankruptcy prevented the company from being ruined by the misstep.

While reasonable minds can disagree on the ethics or risk associated with the sales system employed by Arbonne's field, the critical learning is that the board failed to properly understand and account for the essential role of the sales system. They did not understand that you cannot disrupt or stop a field from using a sales system unless you work with them to replace it with another equally effective one. Without exception, when a sales system is stopped, and no thought is given to its replacement, sales begin to decline rapidly.

The Arbonne example is not a 'one-off.' In fact, I learned this lesson early in my career at USANA Health Sciences, where we had a sales force that was leading with our core vitamin and mineral product called the Essentials. The company's founder was a scientist, and the story told by our distributors all led to the Essentials. We became convinced that we needed a skincare line and launched a very good line with a tie-in to the company's science-based founding. The line initially sold out as current distributors and customers ordered the product to sample it for themselves and their family. To make sure we could keep up with demand, we acquired a manufacturer to make the product for us. But in the end, it never grew beyond the current base and never became a significant seller. The entire line made up less than ten percent of sales, and the field struggled to find any new customers for any of our products until they decided to ignore the new skincare line and to go back to the system they had been using which was centered in telling the story they knew about the Essentials.

I believe that one of the most common causes of a company losing momentum and entering decline is due to self-inflicted confusion caused when the company introduces a product, program or promotion that does not support the system field leaders have been using to grow their business. My goal is to keep you from being the ignorant executive who innocently throws a stick in the spokes of your field's bike and stops their momentum.

SYSTEMS ARE THE IDEAL COMPLIANCE STRATEGY

As we go to press with the first writing of this book, direct sellers are concerned about their future because of the aggressive regulatory actions of the Federal Trade Commission (FTC). Many companies have stepped up their compliance department by hiring more and more auditors, but few have focused on the benefits of solid systems that provide distributors the tools and language they need to represent the company in an ethical and compliant manner.

Distributors want to be compliant with company policies, and they also want to be successful. What better way to assure both outcomes than to create a system that provides your distributors a process for consistently acquiring customers and upgrading many to distributors in a manner you and regulators will be happy with?

ALIGNING EXECUTIVES AND FIELD LEADERS

Unfortunately, unlike the executives of franchise companies, too few direct selling companies understand the critical role of systems. They don't understand that their systems should be central to all they do. In fact, the company's systems should govern its compensation plan and its product plan.

Some executives actually believe systems are all bad—that they are tools used to manipulate, which can be true if a company doesn't own their system and make sure it is a true reflection of the company's culture and values. Other executives erroneously dismiss the use of systems by arguing, "We are a product-focused company and don't need systems." The truth is that product-focused companies (which should be every company) need systems even more so than opportunity companies. Great systems keep distributors focused on the product first and keeps them from adopting an opportunity approach to growth.

I have found that there is great power when a company's executive team understands the value of systems and works with their field to define systems that align with a company's core values.

This book is designed to provide a common vocabulary and to help executives gain a broad understanding of the type of systems their company should have in order to empower the success of their field. My goal in writing the book is to teach top field leaders and executives how to use the principles employed by franchising to ignite hypergrowth by deploying sound systems. I will have been successful if readers learn how to deploy at least one of the eight systems your field leaders need to empower their growth and scale their success.

CHAPTER 2: THE EIGHT SYSTEMS THAT IGNITE GROWTH

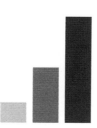

The eight systems we will explore in greater detail in the pages to come are actually not well-kept secrets. In fact, most successful field leaders are well aware of most of the systems we will discuss, but for some reason, even the idea of systems continues to be a well-kept secret among direct selling executives. Even those who believe in systems often fail to fully exploit all eight systems despite attempting to reward those who produce results consistent with all eight.

When I talk about "systems," I'm talking about a recorded way of accomplishing something that eliminates the need for someone to figure out how to do "it" themselves. Author and educator Eric Worre said that you know you have a great system when "everyone knows it, everyone does it, and it works."

Worre said that "great systems eliminate stress for new distributors. Most new distributors want their sponsor to tell them exactly what to do. When new distributors are taught and believe they can follow a system, they'll take more action." All of us want distributors who will take more action.

I discovered systems accidentally as we grew Team Beachbody from $35 million to $380 million in just three years. Eric Worre, however, helped me by articulating with clarity six specific systems to which I have added two more to make it an even eight. Let's introduce you though to all eight systems, so they are no longer secrets to you.

DIRECT SELLING'S EIGHT SYSTEMS:

1. **Customer Acquisition**—a simple and repeatable way to start a discussion with a prospect and to convince them to make their first purchase.
2. **Distributor Upgrade/Acquisition**—a simple and repeatable way to approach your most enthusiastic customers and convert them into becoming a seller.
3. **New Distributor Training System**—a simple and repeatable way to help a new distributor to make their first sale and earn a commission.
4. **Distributor Advancement System**—a simple and repeatable way of helping new distributors advance to a place of profitability within the compensation system.
5. **Convention Attendance System**—this is all Eric Worre and not something I had discovered on my own. Still, after listening to him, I'm convinced that companies need a system in place to get serious distributors to their annual convention and other events.
6. **Communications System**—a simple and repeatable way to provide ongoing information and training to distributors.
7. **Leadership Development & Training**—a simple and repeatable way to help field leaders to become independent and acquire the business and management skills necessary to lead a large organization and effectively influence their team.

8. **Recognition System**—I owe this insight to Milan Jensen, who reminded me that leaders need a system in place that defines when and how they will recognize the achievements of their team members.

While I've come to believe there is great value in understanding and methodically implementing all of these systems, it is my experience that growth can take place by effectively focusing on the first one: customer acquisition. In fact, I believe that one of the major issues legacy companies face today is that they have grown by focusing first on acquiring distributors. While they know they need to become a product-first company, they haven't taken the time to reinvent their systems and to replace their distributor acquisition system with a customer acquisition system.

I also believe that the work of creating and introducing systems is best done by working closely with willing field leaders and then expanded beyond the leader's team with help from the corporate executive team.

Whether you are the leader of a brand-new company, or a large company looking for ways to expand your growth, a focus on creating and implementing these systems—beginning with your customer acquisition system—can do more to assure your success than almost anything else you can do. In fact, I believe too many new companies focus on their compensation plan before they know what they want their field to do and end up failing to compensate their field for doing the right things. Selling systems (customer acquisition, customer-to-distributor, and new distributor training or onboarding) should be established before compensation systems are created to support them.

In my opinion, new companies should follow the path outlined in the diagram below for optimal success.

Product → Selling System → Compensation Plan

The good news is that you don't have to have all your systems in place and running perfectly before you can start to grow. Start (as we will) with the customer acquisition system, and if you get it right—your company will see improved or new growth.

Before we explore each of these systems, starting with your customer acquisition system, let's make sure we define what a system is not.

SYSTEMS ARE NOT:

- **Compensation Plan Maximization Programs**—When I start talking about systems, too many executives and field leaders begin describing numerical goals like "find two who find two," or "get 3 and yours is free." While it might be helpful to use mathematical and numerical alliterations to illuminate the compensation plan or advancement criteria, systems are much more tactical and provide the actual "how-to" vs. the "what to."
- **Defined as Party Plan or Network Marketing**—While the type of selling you advocate will define the type of systems you will need, a "Party" is not sufficiently specific to be a system that provides the "how-to."

Party Plan systems would start with a host acquisition system like the one Sabrina Langford taught her team. Sabrina would teach all new distributors to:

- "Grab their phone and make a list of 50 names, with categories like; friends, family, soccer moms, volunteers, etc.
- Decide which group they will start with and circle the top 5 names in each category and give them a call, inviting them to host an event!
- Make the call and say: "Hey, I am starting this fun business, and I'd love to get to know you and your friends. You can earn FREE clothes just for hosting an 'in-home pop-up.' Invite 25 friends, have a cold drink of water and fun music!" Would you love to earn FREE clothes?"

- **A Manipulation Tool**—Your systems should reflect the values of your company 100% of the time. However, some individuals and companies do teach systems that use manipulation or deceit like the system I found for a summer sales program (I'm sharing this to teach you what not to do AND to show you a system that teaches new distributors exactly what to do):

OPENER PITCH:

- Hey, I sent one of my guys by from "YOUR COMPANY NAME" did they get in contact with you? (right there you got the homeowner's attention)
    - They will respond "no" 99% of the time. Even if they say "yes," just move on.
- The reason I stopped by is because there have been issues with the false alarms, were you informed about that?
    - Again, they will say, "no." At this point, you have the customer's attention. What you just did was shake them off their biased view that when you just rang their doorbell that

you were not just another salesman. Now that you got their interest, they are in your hands… read on.

- At this point, your opener is done, and you are transitioning into your next step.

STEP 2:

- My company is going to be out here correcting issues with the older alarms starting next week.
- What I am doing is looking for a few homeowners that would be willing to help my company display a sign with our company logo and phone number across it (give them the sign in their hand, and point out the number and logo—don't skip a step, all is important).
    - You just explained to the homeowner what you are doing, but they don't clearly see why. Remember, the key to selling alarms is to make what you are doing clear to the homeowner. I'm talking crystal clear. The second it makes sense to them, there is no real reason why anyone should not want the alarm. Now we need to make clear to them why we are doing what we are doing.
- The purpose of us putting that sign out is: when my sales reps are out here next week selling this new fix to the neighbors, they will easily be able to have a few homes on the block to refer to by pointing to your sign. Does that make sense?
    - Make sure the last sentence is used "does that make sense?" Do not move on to the next step until it makes perfect sense.
- What my company has done as an incentive for helping us advertise our sign in your yard is pay to have an "EQUIPMENT BRAND" security system installed in your home. Does that make sense?

- Every time you say "does that make sense," and they seem hesitant, re-explain your previous steps, so it makes sense to them.
- At this point, they might come up with different things such as:
  - So, you mean this is totally free
  - What is the monthly
  - That is too good to be true
  - What all do I get?
  - Oh…. O.k. sure ya go ahead put the sign up
  - Why me? I am still a little confused.
- You must be confident and revert their question back to the reason why you are giving them the system.
- Remember, the more you practice your pitch, the smoother and better you will be at handling the objections.
- Transition time, here is the end of step 2 and beginning of step 3

STEP 3:

- How many doors do you have entering and exiting your house?
  - Here they will normally say two, not keeping in mind the 3rd door entering into the home from the garage. I use that scenario to my advantage like so:
- You have a door coming into your home from your garage, right? They will, of course, answer yes. I then say… perfect, it makes me feel more comfortable protecting that door for you in the case you leave your garage door open and a burglar comes in from that door.
- By the way, is your back door a slider? That I need to take a look at and show you how we secure it.
  - That is a simple way of getting into a customer's house. I normally explain to them that the back sliding glass door

is where most break-ins occur, in my opinion, due to how secluded homes normally are in the back.

- After explaining to the customer what exactly he/she will be getting and how it will work, he/she will now have built up value in what it is you are selling. This is a high point in your sale, and you should be on your way to the close of the sale.

■ Now that they know what they are getting, they need to know how much they are going to be paying and for how long. Remember, there is no better time to throw in the monitoring charge than now. The reason being that they will easily be able to justify how much they are paying for what they are getting. If it is fresh in their head that they are getting the equipment you just explained to them, including the lifetime warranty, free move, and free installation, their decision to get the alarm will be easier. My last pointer about this step is to make sure you really learn to explain how good the product works. Really up-talk about how the system works. The better you explain to them how it works and show them, the easier it will be for them to justify getting the alarm.

STEP 4:

So, the last, Step 4 (Closing the sale)—This is the easiest and best part of the sale.

■ So, what time will you be home tomorrow? They will respond normally ummm after 3 pm. You never want to immediately respond "ok perfect" or "ok that's great" right away. Instead, stop, think for a second and even say "hmmmm after 3:00?.... Well, let me check with the office to see if we have a slot available after 3, let's go sit at your table so I can get some basic info from ya."

Done. Congrats. You made the sale. From there you are writing up paperwork and getting the customers scheduled in for their install.

Do you feel a little of the slime from that "system?" Then let's show you how to create a system that will work for your newest field rep and allow them to maintain their integrity.

CHAPTER 3: CUSTOMER ACQUISITION SYSTEM

Several years ago, SUCCESS Partners, the publisher of *SUCCESS* magazine and *Direct Selling News*, published a direct selling primer that stated:

> For the last 20 years, every single direct selling company in the U.S. market that has reached $10 million a month in revenue has been focused on a single "hero" product, service or ingredient. While the companies may offer many products, the Core Focus is on one thing.[2]

Whether or not that claim is still 100% accurate, the principle is directionally important to understand. Direct sellers are at best part-time representatives who need a very simple system for engaging new customers.

I asked Paul Adams, a leading consultant to direct sellers and a principal involved in the research done by SUCCESS Partners,

---

[2] *The Core Principles*, SUCCESS Partners, version 1.1, page 8

if he felt that statement was still true today. Adams said that it was true, but with one caveat.

"I think it is the focus on the lead story," he said. "Every company has multiple products, but success boils down to understanding the lead product story that is going to get somebody interested and then keeping an extreme focus on that product story. Simplicity is the difference-maker."

In my experience, a great customer acquisition system involves both a focus on a single product, ingredient or system, and a methodology of engaging with prospects. Single story and a simple system of sharing it leave even the newest of distributors thinking, "I can do that!"

SINGLE-FOCUS "ON-RAMPS"

One example of a simple system was the brilliant social media program created by Younique in the company's early days. Younique created a simple mobile phone application that allowed a distributor to take photos of their face showing one side with their mascara and the other without. Younique salespersons would publish these photos on their social media accounts and would get immediate responses from friends and family wanting to learn more. A few years into the company's success, I had the chance to tour Younique's office and to interview their CEO and co-founder, Derek Maxfield. When I walked into their lobby, I was struck by the number of products on display. I had assumed Younique had only their famous mascara. In my interview with Maxfield that day, I asked how much of their sales came from their mascara versus the other few dozen products they had in their line.

"Our mascara makes up fifty percent of our sales, and the other fifty percent of sales come as a result of our mascara," Derek replied.

In other words, they had made it easy to drive interest using one highly visual product, built a system for sharing that product to introduce new customers to the company, and a second system of selling other products to customers during and after their order of mascara.

At Beachbody, we had reasonable success when our sales agents, called "Coaches," attempted to sell the company's fitness products or its flagship nutrition drink "Shakeology." However, the company's real growth came when we introduced the "Beachbody Challenge." To support the Beachbody Challenge, we simplified the product into a "Challenge Pack" and created a system of attracting new customers using a weight-loss challenge.

Coaches were encouraged to start challenge groups every few weeks and to invite those interested in losing weight and getting in better shape to join their FREE groups. They were given the language to use on social media, via text or a phone call, which went something like this: "A group of us are going to start P90X together on Monday, March 1. If you have thought about losing weight or getting in better shape, we would love for you to join us."

Those who wanted to join the group would then be encouraged to start with a Challenge Pack, which we made sure was the best value for new customers. Not only were Challenge Packs the most affordable way to start for new customers, but it was also the most lucrative thing for our Coaches to sell. Challenge Pack sales were a win for the customer, win for the distributor and win for the company.

That simple system made it easy for new distributors to talk about our products. It gave them language to use to engage customers, and it encouraged a frequency of engaging new customers that created a sense of urgency— "we are starting on x date."

After the introduction of the Beachbody Challenge, growth accelerated at a three-year compound annual growth rate (CAGR) above 70% and a five-year CAGR of more than 50%.

SYSTEMS DRIVE MARKETING AND IMPROVE MARGINS

With a simple sales system in place, Beachbody began to align its marketing, new product cadence, and sales incentives. The company avoided wasted spend on marketing programs and sales promotions that did not work. New products were introduced at predictable intervals that supported both seasonal interests in weight loss and the natural timing built into the selling system. New fitness programs were launched as part of a Challenge Pack that included the same component parts (avoiding new training) and priced at one of three predictable price-points.

In other words, the benefits of focusing on a single customer acquisition system not only empowered the field but also empowered the corporate staff. A unified system improved the effectiveness of corporate initiates and reduced waste. We learned that great systems lead to great corporate margins.

GREAT CUSTOMER ACQUISITION SYSTEMS

Great customer acquisition systems follow a simple formula:

1. **Hero Product**—they are developed around a hero product, ingredient or service.
2. **Answer the question "What should I say?"**—they give their field the exact words to use to start a conversation with a new customer and often use a story that sells the product.
3. Provide a *compelling offer* that makes it tough for a customer to say "no."
4. *Create urgency* that overcomes the customer's natural tendency to wait.

Beachbody is not the only company that has figured out how to use customer acquisition systems. Let's look at a few other examples of companies creating compelling customer acquisition systems using this formula.

It Works!™ became one of the fastest-growing companies in direct selling when it used "Wrap Parties" to introduce customers to its hero wrap product. However, when sales slowed and the product seemed to be attracting few customers, the company pivoted to health and wellness products and eventually discovered a new hero product, a fat-burning coffee brew. Rather than introducing the new hero product and hoping distributors would know how to sell it, the company introduced it with the support of a simple sampling pack. This simple sample pack was such a great system carrier that it even includes the words distributors need to start a conversation: "does your coffee make you skinny?" It Works!™ new hero product came with a complete customer acquisition system that includes:

- *the words* the field should say
- a *compelling sample offer* for customers
- a simple follow-up plan
- a 40% discount for ordering now to *create urgency*

Is it any wonder that It Works!™ began to see double-digit growth again after it introduced their new customer acquisition system? Oh, and a bonus, this time their field is on average about ten years younger than their previous sales force.

It Works!™ Vice President of Sales Kyler Pentecost said, "When your field isn't leading with, 'I can show you how to make more money than ever before,' but they're leading with a product, and they're leading with results, that really gives that authenticity that you need. Then your company's foundation is customers and product that's getting results that they become passionate about, and they choose to keep using it or to start sharing it and making income."

It Works!™ is not alone in employing samples effectively. Prüvit has acquired 1.2 million customers with just 50K distributors using its "10 Day Drink Ketones Challenge." TLC (Total Life Changes) has employed its "Samples You'll Feel!" program to renew its growth and has experienced a 300% increase in their growth in their first five months. Revital U has labeled itself the "Sample First Company." However, I love using the It Works!™ example. It not only shows you the value of the system behind a single hero product, but it shows how a company can employ an excellent system to not only grow a single hero product, but how they can pivot to a new hero product, and grow with a substantially new salesforce just by introducing the new hero product with its own customer acquisition system.

Here are a few examples of a few other effective customer acquisition systems:

1. *Revital U–"The Sampling Company"*–acquires customers with a sample first, 100% Money Back guarantee offer. Brand Influencer's pay a monthly subscription of $29.99 and receive 15 samples over their first 90 days and the company subsidizes future purchased sample credits. Talk about simple, a new BI uses a phone app to send samples and to trigger automated follow-up. The idea is: "giving feels better than selling!"

2. *Younique's "Social Video Demonstrations"*—"Don't take my word for it, look at all the customers who are having noticeable results from our product."

3. *Total Life Change (TLC) "Family System"*—"taste, feel, smell, and experience all the benefits a product has to offer, which typically entices them to want to make a full purchase." TLC believes there is no better way to convert a prospect (Sample Customer) to a tried and true Preferred Customer than through sampling.

4. *Beachbody's "See for Yourself Results"*—"Look at all of the people who are losing weight as a result of my coaching. If you want to lose weight, come join my team, and I'll get you started with the most compelling starter pack!"

5. *Nu Skin's "Before and After Teeth Whitening"*—"Here are my before and after pictures. After using this toothpaste for X days, my teeth are whiter. If you want whiter teeth, DM me."
6. *AdvoCare's "Spark Me!"*—"If you are feeling tired every day and don't seem to have the energy to make it through your afternoon, call me, and I'll give you a FREE three-day sample of Spark. Don't take my word for it, try it and see for yourself."
7. *MONAT Global's "Meet MONAT"*—"Join us for a meetup at (wine bar, bistro). If you have been looking for a great hair care line or a network marketing opportunity, then join me!"

In a webinar broadcast by SUCCESS Partners, Revital U CEO Andy McWilliams explained the key elements of their successful "sample first" approach to direct selling. Here are key bullet points from that interview:

- *Products with noticeable results:* "When we first started we actually designed our products to be sampled first, which means that they give you an effect."
- *Samples make it easier for distributors to get a 'yes':* "Most people say yes when you say will you try a sample or will you try this out? It's got to be something with a low threshold of pain [for distributors], and we decided that giving, rather than selling was the way to go."
- *Money Back Guarantees create a simple path to purchase:* "Because we have a money back guarantee it isn't just the three-day sample, people started looking at the first 30 days as a sample… creating a much, much quicker path to money for our brand influencers."
- *Focus first on real customers:* "We want real customers. We feel like that's the only way to build a residual income."

- *Use technology to guide the distributor:* "Utilizing technology to create a uniform way for someone to get the information for the system that they follow has been one of the biggest advantages."

TEST CUSTOMER ACQUISITION AND CONVERSION

The companies that will have the most effective customer acquisition systems will be those companies that are consistently engaged in testing marketing messages and conversion tools at the corporate level. Wayne Moorehead, Young Living Essential Oil's Chief Marketing Officer, wrote an article for the October 2019 issue of *Direct Selling News* where he said, "We need to be more involved in the customer acquisition process, and the new distributors that are joining today, they're okay with it. They're used to it. Again, they don't think in terms of channel conflict like the distributors of old did. We need to think and act, and market, more like retailers. Develop great content, put a little bit of ad spend behind it and then test, learn, and scale."

BONUS SYSTEM—CUSTOMER REORDER SYSTEM

While we haven't devoted an entire chapter to this system, many companies have found it helpful to have a specific system in place to encourage current customers to purchase more than just their hero product. These systems are often as simple as creating a Facebook group for all current customers, so that distributors can share product promotions and information. Smart companies might consider hiring staff to focus on a customer reorder system and might consider more sophisticated programs like:
- Subscription programs
- New product designed to capture more share of wallet
- Monthly product promotions designed specifically to be shared with current customers with the goal of introducing them to new products

WARNING

Please be careful not to turn your field into promotion-based sellers. I've seen companies lean into promotions so heavily that their field begins spending most of their time executing the promotions. The wise company will limit their distributors' focus on existing customers to approximately 10% of their time so they can spend 50% of their time focused on acquiring new customers and 40% of their time upgrading those customers to be a distributor.

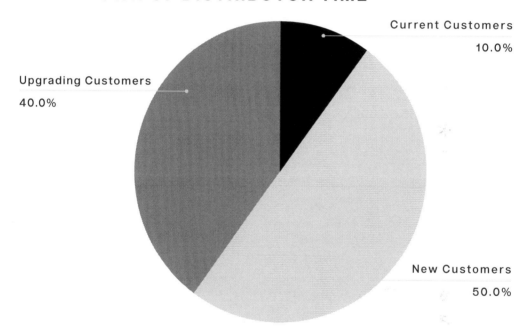

BREAKDOWN OF DISTRIBUTOR TIME

- Current Customers 10.0%
- New Customers 50.0%
- Upgrading Customers 40.0%

As you can see, great systems are bold and simple. The best systems focus on a specific verifiable product benefit. Notice that I'm focused on customer acquisition systems here. Although there are examples of companies that grew primarily with a distributor acquisition system, I believe those days are behind us. While a company needs a great opportunity, the most successful are leading with customer acquisition and then have in place a system for identifying and upgrading their most fanatical customers to be their new distributors. This customer to distributor upgrade system is our next system to discuss.

CHAPTER 4: RECRUITING CUSTOMERS TO BE NEW DISTRIBUTORS

When Amway, Melaleuca, Nu Skin, and Herbalife found their first wave of success in the United States, they were primarily selling a "business opportunity." Their business opportunity message was shared in an environment where the term "side-hustle" hadn't yet been invented. The internet's evolution has brought with it endless opportunities for solo entrepreneurs. While millions are still looking for a way to earn extra income, it is less compelling to join a company just because it offers you the opportunity to earn part-time and then full-time income.

Today's direct selling success stories are focused on first convincing prospects of their consumer value, and then helping them to see how they can earn by sharing those products with others. This evolution not only shows the channel's responsiveness to current regulatory guidance and market opportunities, but it also lends itself to a long-lasting business. In time, companies that focus on opportunity find it increasingly difficult to deliver on their distributor income promises. However, it is not difficult for companies with great products to continue to meet their customers' expectations and to have loyal customers who generate revenues to, in turn, keep distributors earning for years to come.

THE NATURAL CYCLE OF SHARING

For many years, I have been teaching field leaders how important it is to allow customers to naturally evolve into someone who wants to share the product as a distributor. I believe it is unnatural to try to sell a product effectively or to share it with others before you have learned to love it yourself. Conversely, if you love a product, place, or service it is natural to want to share it with others. When friends come to Gilbert, Arizona, I naturally tell them about my favorite sushi restaurant (Temari's), my favorite ice cream store (Handels) and my favorite grocery store (Trader Joe's).

The goal of a great direct selling company should be to attract customers, delight those customers with their product and service, and then find a way to identify and invite those loyal fans to share their enthusiasm for your product with others.

Prüvit has created just a system. Prüvit invites customers to earn Prüvit Bucks for free product by referring two people BEFORE they become a distributor (or promoter). Those who start to refer others or who are talking about the products with others are then invited to learn how to earn commissions for their referrals.

Beachbody's challenge system was understood by Coaches and became an engine of growth because Coaches had a "copy and paste" system to follow to achieve sales, AND it made it easy to recruit new Coaches. Coaches were taught to simply listen for customers who talked about being asked if they lost weight and were given language to turn those conversations into recruiting opportunities. Coaches were taught to ask customers, "Have you ever thought of doing what

I do?" Thus, we were able to create natural recruiting conversations by responding to the conversations that naturally accord because of customers' weight loss results.

Sabrina Langford was one of the first to enroll as a distributor for a clothing direct seller because she loved the product and loved selling it. She grew a large organization and won almost every sales contest, but she didn't think of herself as a great recruiter. I interviewed Sabrina and asked her what advice she would give me if I came to her and told her I wanted to build a team. Sabrina said, "Find your best customers, someone who really loves the product and ask them if they're interested in a business opportunity."

Your best distributors will first be your best customers, but not all of these customers will decide to become distributors without some prompting by current distributors. I have found that there are many direct selling companies without customer acquisition systems, but there are also many with great customer acquisition systems and no system for upgrading customers to be distributors. To grow, you need both.

What makes a great customer-to-distributor system?
1. *It shows distributors what to look for*—at Beachbody, it was someone who had been asked, "what are you doing to lose weight?" At party plan companies, it is customers who attend multiple home shows, place large orders or shop for friends.
2. *It gives recruiters a simple question to ask*—like "Would you like to learn how to earn money for telling others about the product?" or "Have you ever thought of doing what I'm doing?"
3. *It gives customers clear benefits for upgrading*— an additional discount and free shipping are two benefits beyond the opportunity to earn that makes upgrading an easy "yes."

CREATING A PATH TO DISTRIBUTOR

Several companies have decided that there should be interim roles along the path to become a distributor. For example, companies have created:

- Preferred Customer Programs
- Subscription Customers
- Party Host
- Sharing Incentives—some companies have offered product credits, free shipping or future discounts to customers who share their products with others.

These interim roles can help identify loyal customers and allow distributors to see those who are already behaving like distributors. Great distributor acquisition systems will provide current distributors guidance as to when to approach those who are in upgraded customer programs and give them the words to use to invite them to enjoy all of the benefits of being a distributor.

As is the case with many social programs, success breeds success. There is nothing that will help your distributor recruiting efforts more than the stories of success and genuine enthusiasm that are told by those having success. Once you have upgraded a customer to a distributor, you need to make sure you have a system to ensure you deliver on these new distributors' expectations.

CELEBRATING "THE DISTRIBUTOR" AS A DESTINATION

In preparing to publish this book, I sent it to several field leaders whom I respect and was surprised that more than one of those leaders asked me to remind executives how important their distributors are to the company's health. Perhaps in today's movement to remind companies to be customer-centric, we've failed to remember that our distributors are the engine of any direct selling company.

In the words of one experienced field leader: "We know from other friends across the industry that there a lot of front offices that put a number of things ahead of the distributor's needs... it might be wise to give the executives a heads-up that the field knows when they aren't first, and it's not good."

In recalling the culture of a previous direct selling company, Kevin Jensen said, "You know a CEO values the field leader/corporate leader relationship when he instills a field first culture and then backs it up by walking out of important strategy meetings to take unscheduled incoming calls from field leaders and expects other senior executives to do the same if the situation arises. During my time at Nature's Sunshine Products, Alan Kennedy demonstrated his trust by flying field leaders into our quarterly company staff meetings and asking them to share customer success stories so that employees felt a connection to the role they played in distributor success. We knew that the distributors were the most important thing for our company."

One of direct selling's legendary leaders and company owner Rudy Revak is known to have been willing to fire executives who spoke in any way that showed a lack of respect for field leaders.

Perhaps more distributors would recruit, and more customers would upgrade to distributor if it were clear to everyone that we are customer-centric, but no one is appreciated and celebrated and respected more than our distributors.

DATA DRIVEN DISTRIBUTOR SYSTEMS

A few years ago, Roger Barnett the CEO of Shaklee spoke at a SUCCESS Partners University on the opportunity for direct sellers to combine the power of algorithms with the power of personal touch. Today several companies are effectively deploying advanced tools to help their distributors deliver the right message to the right prospect at the right time.

New U Life not only created video content designed to generate interest in being a distributor, to share the opportunity, but also created both automated follow-up and scripts new distributors use to follow up with those who viewed the content. Their content is good and getting better because it is driven by the power of data. New U Life's app not only helps them know who is sharing, but it also tells them how often it is being shared, how often it is being viewed and most important the conversion rate of each message. Over time, they are able to test new content and continue to replace content with messages that are shared more often and have a higher conversion rate among those who are viewing the content.

During an interview for a SUCCESS Partners webinar, Andy McWilliams, the CEO of Revital U, said that the first thing their distributors do is download their app "so we see everything. We believe in data, big data. Three and a half years ago when we were coming up with this idea, we were thinking what would happen if somebody applied all the big data that the big retail companies and other industries are using to really guide their actions and their decision making to our direct sales company? We have so many data points it's insane… It is the future of our business. The magic here is that we don't lose the personal touch of it, relationships are still the thing that makes us who we are. But when you can use technology to enhance it, and to leverage that action. Well, I just think it's the future of the business of our industry."

Not only are companies deploying systems that make it easier for distributors to identify which customers are ready to become distributors, but they are also providing their distributors better and better content to do the "selling" for them, and with automated messaging and tested human scripts to improve their effectiveness.

CHAPTER 5: NEW DISTRIBUTOR SUCCESS SYSTEM

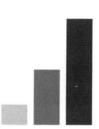

When I began my career in direct selling in the early 1990s, it was a best practice for a company to offer a large starter kit filled with products, videos, company recognition magazines, and a large training binder. These kits were a required purchase for every new distributor, and companies spent considerable time trying to create the perfect kit and the perfect training binder to put in each kit. Companies seemed to believe that their training programs were only limited by the company's imagination. Companies would include videos that were up to an hour long and binders with dozens of chapters on topics as diverse as "making your list" to "meeting new people."

Over the years, fewer and fewer companies require the purchase of a starter kit, and most companies have moved their training online. Training has gone from hours and pages to minutes and paragraphs. Companies are more and more aware of how little time they will be given by new distributors, and so their training becomes more and more refined to include only the most critical and basic training.

I believe the competition for the time and attention of new distributors requires direct selling executives to have a clear and well-defined objective for the training offered to new distributors, and that objective is not "orientation." Let them figure out how to use their back office, call customer service, etc., and instead focus on one critical measure of success: "earning their first sales commission."

In other words, I believe your distributor onboarding system should be measured with one KPI: *"How many new distributors close a sale within their first 3 days?"*

Create a system with that focus, measure and track your results, tweak it from time-to-time, and watch your KPI to see if your tweak improved the number of distributors closing a sale in the first 3 days or not.

Why start out so simple? According to research conducted by one of the InfoTrax as reported by SUCCESS Partners in their recent publication *The Core Principles*, approximately 70% of all new distributors NEVER sponsor or sell a product to anyone. If you want to have a big impact on your business, imagine what would happen if you could change that statistic and instead have 70% of your distributors with a product sale immediately.

While many distributors join companies with the expectation of earning a few hundred dollars a month or to replace their full-time income over time, during my early days in the industry, Melaleuca would print and mail checks of less than $3 to thousands of distributors every month. Many would argue that the cost of printing, preparing, and postage for a single check was more than the value of many of those checks. However, Melaleuca's founder Frank VanderSloot would eventually built a billion-dollar a year business because he understood the impact a simple, though small, check had in retaining new distributors and providing them a reason to continue to build.

The other reason for starting out with a goal as simple as a single sell is that the goal will help you narrow and simplify the initial training you provide new distributors. How do you decide if a piece of information should be included in your onboarding training system? By answering the question, "Does the distributor absolutely need to know this to make their first sale?"

This simple goal also makes it easier for the system creators to outline every single step in the process and then empower each step with instructions and language needed to accomplish each step.

Neora, formerly known as Nerium, experienced explosive growth by providing their promoters with a simple system to earn their first sale. Neora would provide full product samples in their starter kits and teach their distributors to drop off a full bottle of Nerium AD to a friend or family member using six simple steps to earn a sale (see the short training video one promoter created here: http://bit.ly/neriumexample).

1. *Show the Product*—share before and after photos with your friends on social media/text and ask them if they would like to try a free sample for five days. Don't worry if someone asks you questions, just answer any question with "I don't know, all I know is that it makes my skin feel so soft."
2. *Snap it*—before you give them the product, tell them you want to take their picture so you have a "before picture" and set their expectation that in five days, they may not start to see results, but they will feel the results.
3. *Give them the sample*—preferably with your contact information on a label attached to the product.
4. *Plan to get it back*—put a reminder in your calendar. Tell them, "I have others who want to try this sample, so I need to get it back as soon as the five days are over. Today is Wednesday; I'm going to come by and pick it up on Monday."
5. *Check it*—On Monday, go back and pick it up, take their after picture and put it next to the before picture, and show them the results.

6. *Get it back*—give them their before and after picture and ask them if they would like to purchase a product so they can keep using it. Make sure they know there is a full money-back guarantee so they can get a refund at any time.

Revital U not only has a simple customer acquisition system, but the app that powers the sampling system also makes it simple for Brand Influencers to get started. The app gives provides a path to success and is complemented by a compensation plan entirely focused on showing Brand Influencers how to earn their first check quickly. Revital U makes it very simple, subscribe to their Virtual Office for $29.99 a month with no contract, acquire 3 customers and earn $50 plus 2 more for a total of 5 customers and earn another $50! The math makes the goal simple, but the power is in the company-subsidized samples and the app that makes it not only easy to send the samples, but it automates the follow-up.

Total Life Changes Chief Operating Officer John Licari described the company's system for new distributor success in a webinar aired by SUCCESS Partners. Licari described their system in three steps:

(1) *Send Out Ten Samples:* "Every single person who decides to start as a Total Life Changes distributor gets 10 samples. The very first thing we want you to do is send 10 samples, we don't want you to do anything else but to send those 10 samples. We want you to use them wisely. We don't want you to just send them out and hope that the people call you back. You know, we want you to let people know you are sending them a sample."

(2) *Find Five Customers:* "Then step two, we challenge them—and this has been huge for us—and we actually give an extra bonus when they get five brand new customers in their first 30 days. So, get five customers in 30 days and we will give you an extra bonus on top of the retail commissions that you're already going to earn."

(3) ***Find Two Customers to Join You as a Distributor:*** "Then we teach you how to sort the people that have come into your book of business through customer acquisition and see if you can find two people who are willing to do this business with you. And if they join your team, don't teach them anything but sending those 10 samples, getting those five customers and start sorting and seeing if there's two people that might want to do this business with them. It's simple, it's easy to understand."

Licari said, "because of the lower skill set that's needed to learn, people can earn money while they learn the rest."

The ideal onboarding system doesn't require a long training video or a large binder. It is simple to explain, can be printed on one piece of paper, and explained in less than 10 minutes using video. It also can be duplicated over and over again after the initial sale to produce dozens and eventually hundreds of sales. It also does not teach distributors how to sponsor other distributors. The skill of sponsoring is part of your distributor advancement system which we will introduce you to in the next chapter.

CHAPTER 6: DISTRIBUTOR ADVANCEMENT OR ROI RANK SYSTEM

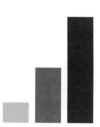

Once a distributor has made their first sale, earned their first commission, and has proven that they can duplicate that success, they are ready to be introduced to the company's distributor advancement system or what I call their ROI (return on investment) Rank system. The ROI Rank system is a simple and repeatable way of helping new distributors advance to a place of profitability within the compensation plan.

The goal of the ROI Rank system is typically defined by a rank in the compensation system, one that allows a distributor to be earning a specific amount (e.g. $500 a month, enough to cover the cost of their own products and any expenses). You decide on the rank based on the earning goal you think is sufficient to lock in the distributor and keep them involved for years to come. This system is your retention system, it provides security for you and your field leaders, and it should be simple to convince your field leaders to focus on this system and to help others use the system to reach the stated rank or earning goal.

This is a system that might include a mathematical formula, and creating something with alliteration might help others remember the objective required to reach the goal. Too often, companies and leaders assume new distributors understand the compensation plan and know what to do to meet the requirements. Don't assume but instead use examples and visuals to make sure you are super clear in explaining the requirements. Even if you don't have a great system in place for getting to your ROI Rank, there is power in creating clarity around the requirements for new distributors.

In the summer of 2019, I was invited to attend the Younique annual convention as a guest of the founders. I attended all the general sessions and selected a few breakout sessions, but the most memorable breakout was taught by Savannah Moore, a field leader for Younique, who taught us how to create a "PINK Factory." Pink is the ROI Rank at Younique and a building block to help top leaders rank advance. Savannah's system for building Pinks was simple:

1. *Recognize Activity*—For example, you might consider recognizing those who make their first sale in 72 hours and repeat with their second shortly thereafter. Savannah taught, "find something to recognize and let them respond."
2. *Invite Them to a "Block Group"*—If and when a person responds, you invite them to join a special "Block Group"—in this case administered on Facebook.
3. *Create Excitement*—As team members join the group, you begin by showing excitement around the ROI Rank. Savannah's goal was to make PINK status a very big deal.
4. *Set High Expectations*—Members must commit to checking in every day and be willing to act on the assignments they are given. Participants will be expected to like and/or comment every day.
5. *Share Success Stories and Invitations to Act Every Day*—Members of the group will be given assignments to help them begin to

meet the requirements on their path to PINK. The assignments will start by repeating the onboarding system and selling to more customers, then use the customer to distributor system to upgrade customers to distributor, and then the onboard system to help their new distributors find and make their first sale.
6. *Celebrate Success*—publicly recognize those who act within the group so that others see that those who act are having success.

Advancement systems are more complicated than any of the systems we have introduced in prior chapters and as you can see by Savannah's PINK Factory, they require more of a structure of support and step-by-step training. The ideal advancement system will use the prior systems as building blocks. This system will show distributors how to put the previous systems together and duplicate themselves by helping others successfully use the systems to advance. If it is difficult for distributors to reach your ROI Rank by successfully duplicating the previous systems, your success will be limited, and you should stop and rethink the rank you've selected, the rank requirements, or systems.

Your requirements will ideally build on the activities of previous systems. Here is an example, "help three people upgrade to a distributor, help two of those new distributors acquire their first customer and help one of those successful distributors to upgrade one customer to a distributor and you win."

A great distributor advancement system will include a method of:
1. *Identifying* those who are motivated to grow a business
2. *Recruiting* participants
3. *Communicating and supporting* participants over a period of several weeks
4. *Assignments, invitations, and challenges* that lead participants step-by-step to the rank advancement.

5. *Celebrating the success* of participants along the way and as they achieve the rank.

Recently I interviewed two field leaders who had helped a nutrition company significantly increase their sales by launching a direct selling division. These leaders talked with me about their challenge in trying to keep their newly enrolled leaders active despite the fact that the company's sales had grown by triple digits in the eight months since they launched into direct selling. The company's executive team was elated by their early success and shocked to learn that their field was not convinced that this company would be their long-term home.

Company executives can avoid this disconnect and significantly improve their chances of success by using advancements to an ROI Rank as one of their Key Performance Indicators (KPI). Even if you haven't yet had the time and resources to create a system to reach the ROI Rank, measuring it will give the company clarity around whether or not they are building a sustainable business or one that will pop and drop. Figuring out both how to reward distributors in a reasonable way to make sure they are seeing a return on their investment and have a profitable business, and working with other field leaders to create the system of support to reach that rank, is critical in building the foundation of an enduring company.

VITAL BEHAVIORS

As you engage distributors on the path to their ROI Rank, it is essential to engage them daily in the behaviors that will lead them to success. While at Beachbody, I became convinced that there were vital behaviors that would eventually lead distributors to success if they did them every day. For Beachbody, the Vital Behaviors were:

1. *Invite, Invite, Invite*—invite someone to try a product or join a challenge group every day. We recommended at least 2 invitations each day.
2. *Be Proof the Product Works*—essential to follow a fitness program and get in shape so that others would see you as a credible Coach, and
3. *Personal Development*—I became a convert to the idea that successful distributors must be investing in their growth (both emotional strength and selling/online skills) every day.

I believe behavior one and three are vital behaviors for every distributor in every company, and you'll have to decide what your company's third vital behavior is. Still, I recommend you discover it and introduce your field to your company's vital behaviors.

CHAPTER 7: CONVENTION ATTENDANCE SYSTEM

Up to this point, we have focused on systems that follow sequentially and have a direct impact on the success of a new distributor. Now we will turn our attention to a few systems that are designed to impact the masses but have no defined place on the timeline of a distributor. The first system we will discuss is not one that I had identified. This was all taught to me by author and educator Eric Worre. After listening to him and personally seeing the result of a convention attendance system he implemented for a company, I'm convinced that companies need a system in place to get serious distributors to their annual convention.

Before we talk about what a convention attendance system looks like, let's talk about the benefits of a packed convention to both the company, its leaders and to new distributors who attend. Recently, I had the opportunity to work with a company that had experienced significant growth followed by a significant decline. They were preparing for a convention that would be the first major gathering since the field leaders had noticed a meaningful decline in their earnings.

Company executives were understandably nervous about the mood of those attending the convention and even more concerned about the early registration numbers which were much lower than previous conventions.

Fortunately, this company's leaders had attended an event and were taught by Eric Worre how to implement a convention attendance system. In the months leading up to the convention, the leaders began to implement what they had learned (with the help from the company) and all showed up to the convention to find 'record attendance' and lots of new distributors. Needless to say, the mood at the convention was electric. Many distributors came to the convention wondering what to expect, and fortunately for this company, the record attendance and the energy from new distributors restored hope and bought the company more time to figure out how to deliver real growth.

Worre claims that learning how to promote an event through a system is the highest paying skill a field learn can learn. According to Worre, leaders will earn, on average, $1,000 per year for every person on their team who attends an event. I do not know how he came up with that number, nor can I find data to provide a quantitative argument to justify the benefit of conventions for the average distributor. However, the money spent by direct selling companies for events is the single largest controllable expense found on their P&L—typically by a significant margin to item number two.

At Beachbody, we were able to leverage our convention to turn summer months after the convention from the least productive to one of the most productive months of the year. During AdvoCare's hypergrowth, the company was absolutely committed to having two conventions (called Success School) each year, and leaders knew how to use those events to maintain sales momentum.

If your company believes in events and is willing to spend the money required to make them great, then how do you make sure the room is full. Nothing destroys hope and momentum more than a convention room that is half empty.

Most event attendance systems rely on a few key tactics:

1. *Leaders directly inviting team members to join their team.*
2. *Leaders purchasing a pack of tickets and reselling them to team members*—Allowing leaders to purchase packs of tickets on sale and reselling those tickets is one great way to engage the leaders. I am partial to allowing them to return unsold tickets so that they don't take a financial hit if they fail to sell all of their tickets.
3. *Preselling the Next Convention*—I found that the best time to sell tickets to the next event is when the field is at an event or watching content from an event on social media and wishing they we there.
4. *Social Content From the Event*—Wise companies and leaders are constantly creating content that shows how much those at home are missing out on.
5. *Deadlines*—Using deadlines to drive urgency will help your field leaders by giving them natural reasons to follow up with their team members who are on the fence. Create deadlines to register with bulk tickets, deadlines for price breaks, hotel deadlines and deadlines to be able to attend exclusive events. The more deadlines, the more times a leader can reach out and promote and talk about the event.
6. *Leaders committed to bringing at least x (typically 10) team members* with them next time. I started with the concept of leaders, but I have to end with it as well because nothing is more important than having leaders who are committed to driving more of their team members and who engage their leaders to commit to bringing a specific number. In other words, your event system might be as simple as making available a 10 pack of tickets with an availability deadline and committing your leaders to sell one

10 pack each. When leaders care and actually sell tickets to their team, attendance increases.

Like some of you, there was a point in my career when I started to convince myself that the days of large meetings were behind us, or that only the companies with a culture of hype could get 7-12K people to attend a convention. After listening to Eric Worre's training and watching the results in a mainstream company (who was in decline at the time), I'm now convinced I was wrong. I now believe that the reason event attendance was not where it should have been in some of the companies I led was that we were not committed to an event attendance system. We wrote the check for these events (big ones), but we didn't have a system that would fill the seats, and our leaders certainly weren't engaged like they should have been. Please don't make my mistake if you are leading a direct selling company or team.

If you are a meeting attendance skeptic like I was, I challenge you to take the time to work with your field to create an event attendance system and prove yourself wrong! You'll never be so happy to be wrong.

WORD TO THE WISE: CONTENT IS KING

It should go without saying that no system will be successful if the content of your event is not compelling and useful to your field. No amount of promotion can overcome poor content. If you have a question about the quality of your content, ask your field. I've yet to find a field leader who would give their honest input when it came to events. You should also attend or invite your staff to attend other company conventions. You can buy a ticket and sneak in, or you can just pick up the phone and offer to exchange convention tickets with a competitor. Most of the companies in the industry will be happy to host you as their guest for the chance to attend your convention in the future.

CHAPTER 8: COMMUNICATIONS SYSTEM

When I joined Origami Owl and had the chance to listen to the company's field leaders for the first time, I was surprised to hear them express their disappointment in the company's poor communication. I was surprised because I knew the company was engaging multiple channels of communication, and it felt like we were communicating all the time. As I pushed these leaders to try to better understand their concerns, it became clear that it wasn't the quantity of communication that was the problem but the lack of a communication cadence. The field didn't necessarily need more information, but they were always afraid that they would miss something. In other words, we might launch a new program on our Facebook page one week and announce a new product on our YouTube channel the next. Leaders wanted to know exactly when and where to tune in for each type of communication. They didn't want to be responsible for monitoring every channel the company was using.

A study published in 2016 in *Nature Communications* and summarized in *The Guardian* by Marc Lewis found that "uncertainty is even more stressful than knowing something bad is definitely going to happen."[3] When we create uncertainty for our field—even when the uncertainty is intended to be something we think will help their business—we increase our sellers' stress levels. Our business becomes complex or difficult for them.

You create certainty, reduce stress and improve productivity when you have a communication system that follows a predictable cadence or pattern of communications. Great communications systems employ consistency around when and how often you will launch new products, promotions, or incentives, when and how you will recognize leaders and when and how you will share new announcements.

Companies should have a communication system that includes a cadence or frequency of communication. A great communication system starts by answering the questions:

1. *"What do we communicate to the field?"* Things like training, inspirational stories, policy changes, new products, promotions, advancements, and recognition, etc.
2. *"Who do we communicate with?"* You will find that some information is suitable for general release, some should be communicated first to field leaders and then from them to their teams, and other information is better communicated only to leaders. Getting clarity about the type of information that goes to your separate audiences and building a plan for each audience is best practice.
3. *"When and how frequently should we communicate?"* Again, this question could be broken down by content (examples listed above) but should also have built-in "opportunity." For example, one of Walmart's competitive advantages is a shift meeting they hold for employees of each department at the beginning of each shift. Walmart doesn't always have critical content to share in the shift meetings every day. Yet, the meetings have

---

[3] https://www.theguardian.com/commentisfree/2016/apr/04/uncertainty-stressful-research-neuroscience

become an advantage because when they do have time-sensitive information to relay, they already have a mechanism in place to ensure all employees receive it from a trusted source within 24 hours.

So, as you plan your cadence with your field, make sure you build in some flexibility and have a mechanism in place that allows you a method of communicating with them on short notice.

4. *"What channel will you use to communicate?"* We have so many options for communication today. From video conferencing to text messaging to good old-fashioned telephone conferencing to newsletters… you'll find that your field has preferences. You might choose different channels for different messages, and that might be driven in part by the audience (e.g. senior leaders vs. all sellers). Whichever channel you choose is important, but even more important is to be consistent in using that channel to communicate specific types of information.

Whether you choose to do a weekly call, an email newsletter, a ZOOM meeting for top leaders or a weekly blog post, work with your field to simplify and standardize the way and the frequency you communicate and teach your leaders to do the same thing with their teams.

LEVERAGING TECHNOLOGY

Gone are the days of sending every message to every person, today's technology allows companies to fine-tune messages and deliver messages to the exact right audience at the exact right time. For example, not long ago I answered a phone call from a number I did not recognize from a local area code and was surprised by the technology being deployed in that call. On the other end of the line was the voice of our local U.S. congressman introducing himself and inviting me to stay on the line to join a live audio townhall starting right then. I had been identified as a constituent of this U.S. congressman and was being invited to a meeting not in the future but right then.

New U Life has learned to effectively push notifications to its field using an app which offers them to ability to geo-target a message and invite distributors to a meeting being held in or nearby their hometown. In an interview with SUCCESS Partners, New U Life VP of Marketing Jeremy Wardle explained this technology. "The cool component in the app is geo targeting built within. If we're going out to Oklahoma, Baltimore, South Carolina, North Carolina, etc., we post the events and the field living in those areas are peppered throughout the week with notifications via the app, as reminders. We could give a 24-hour notice."

CHAPTER 9: LEADERSHIP DEVELOPMENT & TRAINING SYSTEMS

While conducting interviews and research for my first book *Private Equity Investing in Direct Selling*, I was fascinated to see how consistently hypergrowth turned into decline. Direct selling companies tend to have solid and often significant growth for 3-7 years and inevitably see less than a year of slow growth before sales begin to decline.

While discussing this pattern with Darren Jensen, the CEO of LifeVantage, he reminded me of a theory I had also heard Orville Thompson, the CEO of Scentsy, talk about a few years earlier. These CEOs were convinced that companies in hypergrowth fail to develop leaders fast enough to care for all of the new distributors who join the company during that period of time. As the sales team and sales result outpace leadership development, the company eventually sees sales decline until their sales meet the company's leadership capacity.

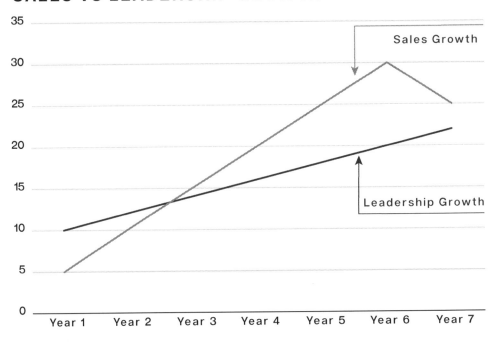

While more and more executives are beginning to understand how important it is to develop their leaders, very few have an actual plan for doing so. I'm guilty of having used "leadership" events to introduce new products, announce changes to the compensation plan and even discuss new selling systems. Still, I did little to actually invest in and build the leaders in the companies I led. If I had to do it over again, I would invest in the personal development of all distributors like eXp Realty has done by sending a copy of *SUCCESS* magazine to each of their active Agent Brokers. *SUCCESS* magazine is a remarkable motivation, inspiration and soft skill education tool that has no direct selling companies or distributor stories or ads to distract your field leaders. I would also put in place a system like a weekly phone call to accelerate the leadership skills of my full-time income earners. Eric Worre taught that "the goal of leadership development is to make dependent leaders independent" with the ability to:

- *Create Action* in their team
- *Remain Focused* on the systems that grow their business—especially during difficult times
- *Build Culture* and stickiness among their team members
- *Solve Problems* on their own, and
- *Communicate Vision* to their team

Milan Jensen, CEO of WomenKind, warned that too often untrained leaders fall into the trap of empathizing with their team when they call to complain about the company, a new product, a promotion or anything else. Milan said we tend to believe that our teams want us to agree with them, when in reality, they want their leader to tell them that everything is going to be OK, or in the words of Worre, "there is a promised land, and we can get there together."

Often, we tend to forget that for many of our leaders—even those with incomes greater than our own—this is their first true leadership experience. While many are "natural born leaders," many of the skills required of field leaders during times of stress (stress from hypergrowth or decline) are not those skills we are naturally born with, but rather they are skills that require experience, training, and practice.

Wise companies will put in place a leadership development system during the good times because they will find it is very difficult for the company to stand in front of leaders and be the "leadership expert" when times are tough. Often, companies who find themselves in a downturn will not be able to use corporate sales executives or other staff to conduct the leadership development training because the field's confidence in them has been impacted by the company's poor performance.

Your leadership development system then is a simple and repeatable way to help field leaders acquire the business and management skills necessary to lead large organizations and effectively influence their team. Many of the skills taught will not require direct selling experience like bookkeeping, handling difficult interpersonal situations and effective speaking and presentation skills. Other topics should be specific, like using systems, maximizing the compensation plan, legal do's and don'ts and promoting events. If I were building a leadership development system, it would include:

1. *Effective Use of Leadership Events*—I would have leadership events that individuals would be required to qualify for each year, and I would protect the agenda to focus on leadership skills with very little other news or distractions.

2. *New Leaders Orientation at the Company Home Office*—Leaders who earned a rank with earnings equivalent to full-time income would be invited to the home office to help strengthen their relationship with key executives and staff and to provide them with a clear expectation of what it means to be a leader in your company.

3. *Leadership ZOOM or Conference Calls with experts*—While it might be very expensive to get top trainers to attend an event, the cost of having an expert on a video or audio conference with your leaders is affordable and worth the investment. If you could get Rita Davenport to teach your field leaders to not complain to their downline, or Dave Taylor to teach the tools of influence, or Eric Worre to teach a one hour course on promoting events, or John Addison to teach the principles of leadership, or Kindra Hall to teach your leaders how to use stories effectively in their meetings and training, or to get Milan Jensen teaching your top leaders how to support one another, you would be well on your way to successfully creating independent leaders.

4. *Personal Development Content for Early Leaders*—In addition to the tools available for your full-time income earners, I would invest in personal development for anyone who has started to build a business. The most affordable tool I'm aware of is *SUCCESS* magazine, which can be personalized with your company cover

on the outside and sent to your young leaders every other month for about $2 per person.
5. *Social Media and Personal Branding Training*—In today's market, top leaders need to understand and to use social media and how to build and protect their personal brand.

Your leadership development system should be well understood and should be on your calendar a year in advance. Don't let your sales outpace your leaders' ability but invest in your leaders early and often and do all you can to make sure your leaders are prepared for whatever may happen. Dedicate the time and use the resources available to you (conference calls, leadership events, etc.) to add curriculum your field leaders might need as you face unexpected turns in the future. Waiting to invest in developing your leaders might cost you millions when time gets tough.

CHAPTER 10: RECOGNITION SYSTEM

Mary Kay Ash is quoted as saying, "There are two things people want more than sex and money… recognition and praise." My experience has taught me over and over again how true that statement is. In fact, in the past I'm quite sure that our field has been more motivated by the recognition and incentives we had in place than the compensation plan we had in place— I'd be willing to bet most didn't understand how our compensation plan worked. Still, they knew what it took to be recognized on stage.

Writing for the website Leaderonomics, Ang Hui Ming said, "In a 2016 survey commissioned by former Yum! Brand's chief executive officer and author David Novak, a staggering 82% of American employees feel they are not recognized enough by their leaders for the contributions that they make." Perhaps this longing for being noticed is why so many distributors stay with companies and field leaders who get recognition right.

Every company should have a basic system in place to recognize the rank advancements of its distributors in support of their compensation plan. In addition to that basic recognition program, the company can layer other recognition tools to help support the systems they implement.

Earlier this week, I met with two excellent field leaders who described how disconnected their company's compensation plan was from the actual systems that were working for them and their team. They took some solace in learning that many companies have the same problem. Most companies create their compensation plan first and then create their other systems. The result is a compensation plan that doesn't exactly reward behaviors and outcomes their selling systems espouse. The good news is that you can create a recognition program to make up the difference.

As soon as you know what systems work and which you want to encourage your field to follow, you should turn your attention to creating a recognition system (which may or may not include any incentives) that showers attention on those who are implementing your systems. If your systems include acquiring new customers via the sales of a special pack, then create a recognition program that highlights those who have sold so many (2-3) every month and another program to recognize the top 3-5 sellers of those packs every month and the top 10 every year.

The best way to ensure the behaviors you want and to begin to get people to use a system is to recognize those who are having success with the system.

In building a recognition system, here are some principles to follow:

- *Use Quantitative Measures and Avoid Qualitative Recognition*—One of the best ways to ruin the effectiveness of a program is to include "qualitative" criteria that leave people guessing if the person really earned the reward or whether or not they are a favorite of the judge(s). Make life simple and reward only those things you can easily measure.

- *Consistency & Cadence*—As soon as possible, make it clear how often you will recognize certain results and when those results will be announced. Random recognition for outstanding results can provide a momentary sense of satisfaction for the person or team recognized, but only rewards that people know are available to be earned with clear deadlines to obtain the rewards will actually drive results.

Too often, companies sit down to plan their convention and say, "what should we recognize on stage this year." If your field doesn't know what it takes to be recognized on stage, then all the money spent on ribbons and rewards will be wasted. Announce next year's on-stage recognition this year and let it be a motivator all year for those who are driven by recognition.

- *Company vs. Team*—Company-wide recognition programs are effective and should be implemented alongside team recognition programs. The ideal program will include recognition for the same activities at both levels. There will be a top reward winner for the company and thousands of top rewards winners for the same activity on the team level.

NOTE: If your field leaders are to be effective in recognizing and rewarding the desired behaviors and results, they will need access to data. For many companies, this requirement can be difficult and often delays implementation because companies think they have to wait for new software or at least for new reports to be made available in their back-office software system. I've found that it's often worth the effort to just hire someone to create and distribute reports to your field leaders until the reports can be automated.

The recognition I'm proposing is not an addition to your compensation plan. While it could include incentive travel or small prizes, it is definitely non-cash recognition. According to a presentation made at a recent Direct Selling Association event, Maritz Travel reported that "non-cash rewards tend to be more effective and more motivating than cash rewards."

The team at Maritz Travel sited Scott Jeffrey's research, which found that "when other people know about your success, you get a strong feeling of social reinforcement. However, it's often not considered acceptable to discuss cash rewards. That makes non-cash rewards a stronger motivator when it comes to social reinforcement." He also learned that "people think about non-cash rewards more frequently, which contributes to higher performance and motivation."

So, the good news is that you can begin to impact performance and can accelerate the adoption of the systems we have outlined in this book with very little or no cash and a little love.

CHAPTER 11: LAUNCHING NEW SYSTEMS

Creating customer acquisition systems (or any of the eight systems we've discussed) is most often a process of discovery rather than of creation. For companies that have sales and thousands of sellers, the process of identifying a new customer acquisition system begins by identifying those individuals and teams who are growing.

During my tenure at Beachbody, I recognized early on that the company's early growth had not come from traditional recruiting and selling activities but from the identification of founding leaders who brought with them some experienced direct sellers who were close to them. The rest of the growth came as a result of leads the company curated for its distributors from its television direct marketing campaigns. Beachbody sold its fitness programs via infomercial and then assigned all of the customers who were upsold Nutritionals by their telesales department to their "distributors." In my interviews with top leaders, I heard stories of receiving checks without knowing how they were earned. When the company discontinued the aggressive lead program, sales in Team Beachbody (their direct sales division) plummeted from a $50 mm+ run rate to a $36 mm run rate.

After traveling to meet with many of the company's top leaders, I began to study the sales results and noticed that many of the top Coaches were using social media despite our sales team's strong opposition to that practice. I reached out to those top Coaches and told them of my interest in learning from them and invited them to the office for a few days of dialogue. I invited each of these sellers to stand and share with the others what they were doing and what they had learned and allowed the others to ask questions. I sat in the back of the room feverishly taking notes and chimed in with my own questions from time to time. Some of the Coaches were more open than others. Most came with concern that the company had called them in to punish them. All left that event having created new allies and having learned from each other. I left the gathering knowing that I had to:

- Choose a System That Could Be Duplicated and Scaled
- Develop a Method of Testing and Refining the System
- Figure Out How to Align the Field Around the New System

Here is what I've learned, and my advice for identifying new systems to support and scale your company.

CHOOSING SYSTEM THAT CAN BE DUPLICATED AND SCALED

As you begin to study the individuals and teams who are having success in your company, it will become clear which ones understand and use systems and which ones are just extraordinary salespersons.

As you study the success of those who are growing their business, your primary objective is to separate success that is the result of a great or extraordinary person from the success that is a result of an extraordinary and simple system. *You are looking for systems, not people,* because you can't duplicate people, but you can plug anyone into a great system, and they will succeed. You can scale with systems faster than you can scale with people.

You can scale with great systems faster than you can scale with great people.

Your first goal in finding a system you can scale is to sort through those already being used in your company and separate the system from the salesperson. At Beachbody, we found several Coaches who were recruiting prospects to Facebook groups and encouraging them to work together to support one another as they all experienced one of our multi-week workout programs. Another leader would start a group every first Monday of each month, and we learned from that leader the power of having an impending deadline. It took us several months to learn and identify best practices and then a few more months to put together what we thought was a system that could be used by a brand-new Coach.

It is possible that there are no effective systems, and, in that case, you will be forced to create your own. You should be able to find best practices from multiple people and piece them together into a system. If that is the case for you, and you were starting with a customer acquisition system, I would start by asking—and using experimentation and actual human-to-human experience—to answer the following questions:

- How does one start a discussion about our products with a potential customer? What are the exact words that come out of the seller's mouth? Are they starting from scratch or putting themselves in front of someone who is already looking for your solution? Systems that fail to give the sellers the words to use to

start a dialogue only work with great conversationalists and fail the "below-average person" test.
- How does one prepare someone to receive an invitation to purchase or try your product? What are the words of the invitation? How do you bundle the invitation with an offer so compelling that the invitation is more likely to be acted upon?

DEVELOP A METHOD OF TESTING AND REFINING THE SYSTEM

Unless your founder is a former distributor with documented and recent success with systems similar to the one you are advocating, most field leaders are understandably skeptical of any selling systems that come from the company. I am among the corporate executives who have been guilty of being arrogant enough to believe I could create and teach field leaders "how to sell" even though I had never sold anything myself. My experience has taught me that when it comes to creating new sales systems, there is no substitute for testing and validation.

Once you have found, refined or created a new system you plan to introduce, you need to find a way to validate that your system works in practice. I believe the best way to validate new systems is to work with leaders who don't have a strong commitment to their own system, are loyal to the company, are willing to trial the system as you've designed it and then work with you to improve it as necessary. Ideally, you want leaders who:

- *Are respected by other leaders*—they can help you sell the system to others if it works.
- *Are actively working*—you want leaders who will deploy your system often, not just once or twice.
- *Are collaborative by nature*—you want leaders who will deploy your system as it was designed (not as they think it should be designed) and then work to improve it from there.
- *Can be trusted to keep secrets*—eventually, you will want the world to know about systems that work, but you don't want someone

who will erode confidence by sharing the inevitable failures you may experience during your testing.

ALIGN THE FIELD AROUND YOUR NEW SYSTEM

Once you have validated the effectiveness of your new system, you will want to introduce it and convince the majority of your field leaders to migrate from the systems they are using to yours. In my experience, it is not reasonable to believe that ALL leaders will migrate and support the new system. I also do not advocate forcing or coercing them to do so. Instead, I've found that the best systems eventually sell themselves. Therefore, my approach to implementing new systems is to delay a large reveal and instead slowly expand your test ... first, as a beta limited to only those teams who will deploy it by giving it their full support. The ideal introduction will take time and will be more of a "pull" than a "push" strategy. As leaders in your beta begin to have success and talk about it, others who are struggling will want to learn how they can deploy the system to their team. Ideally, the system will be old news, and the field will be begging for it by the time it is officially introduced.

Have you heard the saying, "go slow to go fast?" In my opinion, the fastest way to gain adoption is to introduce it slowly and only as others are demanding it.

During the period of alignment, you will have leaders who will criticize the system or argue that there doesn't need to be a single way of accomplishing the goal of the system. This is true, and I believe you can and should verbally support systems taught by successful teams. But you should focus your corporate resources on supporting the system you have introduced if it is delivering results. There are tremendous operational efficiencies and real cash savings when the company commits to supporting a single system.

As we committed to the Challenge system at Beachbody, the company began to align its marketing, new product cadence, and sales incentives. We layered on a recognition system called the "Success Club" that reward Coaches for selling "Challenge Packs" to new customers. New fitness programs were launched as part of a "Challenge Pack" bundle that included the same component parts (no new training!) and priced at one of three predictable price-points, all delivering great value to customers and a strong retail commission for the selling Coach.

It was a great system because everybody knew it, everybody did it, and it worked. This new system became an engine of growth because it required almost no training. Coaches had a "copy and paste" system to follow to achieve sales.

With the Beachbody Challenge as the customer acquisition system, we were able to create a simple customer to a Coach upgrade system. Recruiting new Coaches became simple. Coaches were taught to listen for customers who talked about being asked if they'd lost weight and were given language to turn those conversations into recruiting opportunities with the simple question, "Have you ever thought of doing what I do?"

Our new Coach onboarding system was simple. Because most of our new Coaches had been part of a Challenge Group, they knew exactly what we wanted them to do. Our system for getting to profitability was easy because we engineered the economics of our Challenge Packs to benefit those working our system, and we could easily show the profitability of following it.

Aligning around new systems is not simple. It takes hard work, and I don't think it can be done in less than 18 months, but your company can experience growth as new systems are perfected and introduced. Whatever the cost in trial, error, and patience, the end result is so powerful for a company and its field. I believe there is no better way for a company to spend its time at launch or during a period of renewal. With the exception of a historically few unicorn new products, in my opinion, there is no innovation that can improve results faster than to align around new systems beginning with a powerful customer acquisition system.

CHAPTER 12: MANAGING WITH SYSTEMS

Now you understand how critical systems are to effectively empowering your independent sales force, and the eight systems are no longer secrets to you and your management team. However, to make the most of your systems, you will need to learn to adapt your management and decision making to account for systems.

Early on, you will want to prioritize opportunities and use the implementation of new systems as a primary tool for growth. For example, if you find that your company is enrolling thousands of new customers but are seeing distributor enrollments dry up, you will want to focus your attention on creating or refining your customer to distributor upgrade system. If you are enrolling lots of distributors, but few distributors are selling, you will want to focus your energy on your new distributor onboarding system.

Below are the five steps I would recommend you consider as you begin to learn how systems impact your company and the tools available to grow and to accelerate growth.

STEP 1: ASSIGN RESPONSIBILITY FOR EACH SYSTEM

Even before you implement every system, you will want to make sure you assign responsibility for each of these systems to one or more individuals. It is one thing to have a "training department" with broad responsibility for all things training, and a very different thing to have an individual or individuals who are completely committed to increasing the number of distributors who reach your ROI Rank. Aligning your team's accountability and rewards to those areas that impact the success of your field will pay big dividends and help you from creating products and programs that sound good, but that actually doesn't move the needle.

Even if you are a young company and don't have the staff to assign one person to each system, make sure that there is someone accountable for each system. In other words, if you are the CEO and the head of sales, you might be accountable for all eight systems at first, but as you hire other executives, you might turn all or some of those systems over to them. Accountability might mean prioritizing and focusing on one of the eight now and one in a year from now. You don't have to implement all systems immediately, but you will want someone thinking about these systems and making conscious decisions of when and where to use scarce resources.

STEP 2: IMPLEMENT SYSTEM-BASED KPIS

Now that you are employing systems to empower your field, you will want to start using KPIs designed to tell you how each system is working. Specifically, you will want to measure:

1. *New Customer Enrollments*—and how often those new sales include the hero product or kit that is the focus of your selling system.
2. *New Distributor Enrollments*—you will want to know how many total distributors you're enrolling and how many of your new distributors were formerly your customers.

3. *Percentage of New Distributors Selling*—breaking this down so you can see how many close a sale during their first 72 hours, their first month, and their first 60 and 90 days.
4. *Percentage of Distributors Earning Your ROI Rank*—The best way to determine the strength of your company is to know how many distributors you have who are earning an ROI from their business in a time period they view as acceptable (it will take some research to find out how many days that should be).
5. *Convention Attendance*—It is easy to measure convention attendance, which will help drive your event attendance system, and is to be able to measure the number of team members top leaders have at convention. If you are going to ask leaders to be responsible for getting their team to attend events, then measure their performance and rank them if possible.
6. *Communications Effectiveness*—Measuring the effectiveness of your communication systems takes a little more work but is also worth the effort. Can you measure email opens, attendance on calls/video conferences, likes or engagement on social posts? Charge your communications team with the task of measuring how many people they are reaching and from time-to-time throw in an incentive that will help you measure how many people are actually reading or viewing your content.
7. *Leadership Development System*—Measuring how well you are doing in creating independent leaders might require you to administer a survey or to conduct interviews on a regular frequency. Work with your team to measure how well you are equipping your leaders and provide your training team a way to show their effectiveness and progress.
8. *Measuring Recognition*—Your recognition program should be measured qualitatively (How are we doing recognizing your accomplishments?) and quantitatively (Are those results we are recognizing/rewarding improving?).

STEP 3: RECOGNIZE NEW CONSTRAINTS

Ultimately, having the eight systems in place to empower your field will ignite growth and improve your field's performance, but these systems will also put limits (I would argue healthy limits) on you as a management team. The primary limit for most person-to-person direct selling companies will be that you will want to avoid introducing products that compete for the attention of your hero product/pack. In fact, most new products will be used to feed the system you have in place to encourage reorders from current customers and distributors. If you do come up with a product that should replace your current hero product, you will recognize that it might require that you reinvent your customer acquisition system to support that new hero product like It Works! did.

A strong customer acquisition system should also impact the timeline and the process you use to introduce new products. Many companies believe that new products must be a surprise to distributors until the moment they are introduced, Nu Skin found success with a process that involved distributors years prior to the product's actual introduction.

During his tenure as CEO of Nu Skin, Truman Hunt threw out the long-standing practice of keeping all new products as closely guarded secrets. Nu Skin instead developed a thorough process of allowing qualifying leaders to respond to new product ideas years before they were to be launched. These leaders understood the field's selling systems and knew how to prepare for and adapt their systems to make the most of new products without disrupting those systems. In other words, the new product collaboration was not so much about whether or not the distributors liked the product, but more importantly, included a dialogue about how they could sell the product given the current selling system they were using.

To date, Nu Skin is one of only a few companies that practices this collaborative method of including sales process in their new product development, and to their credit are one of the few companies that has seen incremental sales from new product introductions. The system they use today has been adapted over the years, but they have pioneered a process of collaboration that other companies would do well to learn from and employ.

Once you employ systems, you will also want to employ a new product development process that allows you to work hand-in-hand with your field leaders to create a unified marketing and sharing system that makes it easy for the field and leaves new reps thinking "I can do that!" Before you launch a new product, make sure you and your field leaders are crystal clear in your understanding of how the product will support your existing systems. Today, far too many companies leave the selling system to their independent distributors, and that's to everyone's detriment.

STEP 4: SYSTEM INNOVATION: AN INSTRUMENT FOR GROWTH

Even after you have implemented the eight systems, your work is not over. Just like products, systems need to be refreshed from time to time and can actually be replaced or simply improved, causing renewed growth. Often a company can experience slowed growth and declining field participation because they have failed to innovate and help the field discover a new customer acquisition system. At other times, a perfectly good system can become outdated and will need to be replaced for one of two reasons:

- Field Fatigue
- Social Media/Technology Changes

FIELD FATIGUE

Unlike a manufacturing system that can be deployed and kept in place for decades with only the need for maintenance from time to time, the systems used in direct selling depend on human beings who get fatigued even if the system is working. During my tenure at Beachbody, weight loss "challenges" became popular and Beachbody, AdvoCare, ViSalus and others built very successful customer acquisition systems around them and grew by hundreds of millions of dollars. By the time I joined AdvoCare, "challenges" still worked, but the field leaders were tired of deploying them and were in desperate need of a new system. In other words, there was still confidence in the products, but the field was tired of doing the same thing year after year, and the customer acquisition system was in need of an update. As we began to bring freshness to the customer acquisition system, we began to see renewed energy and participation in the field.

SOCIAL MEDIA/TECHNOLOGY CHANGES

As Facebook moved off of college campuses to become a main street social connection tool, several direct selling companies learned how to do business very effectively on the platform. Younique, Jamberry, Beachbody, and many others saw rapid growth as their field leaders acquired customers on Facebook. While Facebook is still the largest social media platform in terms of total usage, the growth of users and commerce has been migrating to Instagram and YouTube, and few direct sellers have figured out how to adapt or augment their customer acquisitions to these new platforms. Clearly, one of the biggest innovation opportunities awaiting direct sellers is to help distributors identify a system for acquiring customers on new social platforms.

STEP 5: ADD TECHNOLOGY TO ACCELERATE GROWTH

In my opinion, too many companies try to implement new technology as a system for growth. Starting with software and hardware solutions typically force companies to adapt their systems to match the technology's capability. Perhaps this is why so many software implementations fail or have little upside for direct sellers.

I believe technology should be added to the mix after a system has been tested and has been proven to work without the technology. For example, several of the great customer acquisition systems rely on sampling and a few of the most successful sampling companies have added an app to make the process of offering a sample simple. Technology should be a supporting actor that adds acceleration, but rarely should a company let a technology solution direct the "how" they will do business.

SUMMARY

Having good products is important. Finding great leaders can make a world of difference. No start-up will survive without access to cash. These statements are all true, are all understood by executives, and are all part of most start-up plans, but it's my experience that few executive teams have the discipline to also give adequate attention to their customer acquisition system. While I don't think it's feasible to start a new company with all eight systems in place, I also don't think anyone should launch a company without their customer acquisition system in place, tested, and aligned with their hero product, their compensation plan, their marketing and pricing plan, and their rewards and recognition system. I'll repeat that statement one more time for clarity: No direct selling company should open their door without a customer acquisition system.

Now that these eight systems are no longer a secret to you and now that you have a basic understanding of how to implement and manage your company with these systems in place, it's time for you to pick the first system you will implement and begin to ignite your growth.

ACKNOWLEDGMENTS

I wish to acknowledge and express my gratitude for the executives, consultants and friends who have contributed content to this book. I'm especially grateful for the insight gathered from Eric Worre, Milan and Kevin Jensen, and the many field leaders like Jeremiah Captain, Rodell Razor, Sabrina Langford, and so many others I've had the chance to work with in the past.

I'm grateful to Stuart Johnson, CEO of SUCCESS Partners, and the entire design and editorial team at *Direct Selling News*, who provided valuable insight and assistance in getting the book published and in helping me find an audience that can benefit from its contents.

Finally, a special thanks for the love, support and patience of my wife and eternal companion, Erin, whom I love, and our children: Spencer and his wife Maris (the parents of our first grandson, Brooks), Madison, Allison, Sydney and Kate, and to my father and friend Dr. Leon H. Blake.

ABOUT THE AUTHOR

Brett A. Blake is a direct selling veteran having led four companies (both person-to-person and party plan), served as a marketing executive for two others and served on several boards. He has served as the president, CEO or GM of seven companies, both public and private. Brett is the author of *RENEWAL: Leading Direct Selling Turnarounds*, *RENEWAL for Field Leaders*, and *Private Equity Investing in Direct Selling: Identifying Risks & Rewards*. He is a strategy consultant for direct selling companies and has been hired to advise investors on nearly a dozen direct selling transactions. Brett is a personal advisor and coach to CEOs, boards and investors.

In addition to writing and speaking, Brett enjoys mountain biking and spending time with his wife Erin, their six children (one by marriage) and their newborn grandson. Brett will leave his consulting and speaking work beginning in July 2020 because he, Erin and their youngest daughter Kate have been called to lead the Colorado Denver North Mission for the Church of Jesus Christ of Latter-day Saints for three years.

Made in the USA
Monee, IL
03 June 2023

35194957R00058